MW01535313

Published by:
The Mark David Corporation
23 Kelton Court, San Mateo, CA 94403
650-341-6504
www.markdavid.com

Credits:
Compiled by Mark David
Designed by Toby Cowan, Performance Design Group
Coordinated by Deme Jamson
Edited by Dan Zadra, Luana Cowan and Bernie Fischer

Special thanks to:
Janet Davidow, Julie Gentile, Tina Glover, Emily Keyser,
Kevin Kissling, Vivian Lai, Karen Lum

ISBN 978-0-9961424-5-8

Printed in U.S.A. with soy inks.

mark david
releasing human potential

Be Inspired

The quotes in this little book
express some of the best parts
of the human spirit.
May the thoughts in these
pages bring joy and inspiration
to your life, love and work.

—MARK DAVID

"Throw the spotlight into every corner of your company or community and celebrate the people who are doing things right."

**Never squander an opportunity
to tell someone you appreciate them.**

— DIANE WILDE

Be a good-finder.
Try to catch people red-handed
in the act of doing things right—
and praise them for it.

— BILL MEYER

Appreciation is a wonderful thing:
it makes what is excellent
in others belong to us as well.

— VOLTAIRE

When someone does something good, applaud! You will make two people happy.

— SAMUEL GOLDWYN

Among the duties of life, I hardly know any one thing more important than that of praising where praise is due.

— SYDNEY SMITH

The best leaders are coaches appealing to the best in their people; their doors are always open; they are problem solvers, advice givers and cheerleaders.

— ROBERT TOWNSEND

Nothing else can quite substitute for
a few well-chosen, well-timed, sincere words
of praise and appreciation. They're absolutely
free and worth a fortune.

— SAM WALTON

**Be aware of what others are doing,
applaud their efforts, acknowledge their
successes, and encourage them in their
pursuits. When we all help and encourage
one another, everyone wins.**

— JIM STOVALL

**There is no sin in delegating.
The sin is trying to do it all.**

— DEBORAH ROBERTS

What separates those who
achieve from those who do not
is in direct proportion to one's
ability to ask for help.

— DONALD KEOUGH

Even the greatest genius will not
be worth much if he pretends to draw
exclusively from his own resources.

— GOETHE

**There is no such thing as an individual
sport or a sole proprietorship. There are
always a lot of people behind the scenes
for anything great to happen.**

— UNKNOWN

"When people treat them

act heroically, as heroes."

— JEFF GOFORTH

A nation reveals itself not only by the men and women it produces but also by the men and women it honors.

— JOHN F. KENNEDY

Show me the person you honor
and I will know what kind
of person you are.

— THOMAS CARLYLE

The world knows nothing
of its greatest people.

— HENRY TAYLOR

**In our world of 'big names,' legions
of our most creative and courageous
people tend to be anonymous.**

— **DANIEL J. BOORSTIN**

Each day unknown men and women do great deeds, speak great words and suffer noble sorrows.

— CHARLES READE

There are unrecognized heroes among our neighbors, friends and co-workers.

— HAROLD W. BERNARD

Most people aren't appreciated enough, and the bravest things we do in our lives are usually known only to ourselves.

— PEGGY NOONAN

Everyday courage has few witnesses. But yours is no less noble because no drum beats before you, and no crowds shout your name.

— ROBERT LOUIS STEVENSON

**The five most important words:
'You did a great job.'**

— GALE WHITNEY

We all need to be recognized for what
we're doing, for our work. Every once
in a while we need someone to come
up to us and say, 'You're beautiful.
That was well done. That's nice.'

— LEO BUSCAGLIA

We can't all be heroes because
someone has to sit on the curb
and clap as they go by.

— WILL ROGERS

**Truthfully, everyone who does the
best he or she can do, day in and day out,
should be considered a hero.**

— PAT MURPHY

"It's not how much we admire or appreciate someone, it's how much they know it that counts."

— ANDREW LYON

Silent gratitude isn't much use to anyone.

— GLADYS STERN

Many people hesitate to praise and
celebrate the people they work with,
thinking it would seem like flattery.
But the great ones know they are in
a spiral of helping, a contest of giving.

— DALE DAUTEN

Feeling gratitude and not
expressing it is like wrapping
a present and not giving it.

— WILLIAM ARTHUR WARD

**Appreciation can make a day,
even change a life. Your willingness
to put it into words is all that is necessary.**

— MARGARET COUSINS

A proven way to accelerate improvement and progress: reward and celebrate closer and closer approximations of the desired end result.

— ANDREW COMPTON

We can help the marathon runner the most by offering encouragement and nourishment along the entire track, not just by waiting at the finish line with a trophy.

— ALEX HIAM

Encouragement is oxygen to the soul.

— GEORGE ADAMS

**There must've been hundreds
of people cheering at some of those
track meets, but my father's voice always
found me. A simple, 'That's it kid,'
and my feet grew wings.**

— MADISON RILEY

If you think a complimentary thought about someone, don't just think it. Dare to openly compliment people and pass on compliments to them from others.

— CATHERINE PONDER

To every leader and manager:
In the next 96 hours, send four thank-you notes to front-line employees for a job well done; repeat every 96 hours for the rest of your life. Repeat the same process with your customers.

— TOM PETERS

Don't just think it— *ink it!*

— DAN ZADRA

**Put your words in a letter so
they won't die on the empty air.
When someone wins an award, leads
a drive, preaches a great sermon, or
contributes to the greater good of your
company or community, lift their spirits with
a personal note or handwritten letter.**

— W. A. PETERSON

"Give all the

credit away."

— JOHN WOODEN

Morale is self-esteem in action.

— AVERY WEISMAN

Don't be afraid to step on the
victory stand. Win with class and character.
You've worked hard, you've paid the price
and you deserve to be recognized. Just be
sure to share the credit with others.

— HOWARD FERGUSON

In order for me to look good,
everyone around me needs to look good.

— DORIS DRURY

**The most powerful experience
is when someone gives the credit
away to the team for a job well done.
The glow of their achievement warms
the room, and then some.**

— SUSANNE BERGER

**The best thing you can do each day
is to reach out and do things for others.**

— MARK DAVID

There is no exercise better for the heart
than reaching down and lifting people up.

— UNKNOWN

Those who are lifting the world upward and onward are those who encourage more than criticize.

— ELIZABETH HARRISON

Help each other be right, not wrong. Look for ways to make new ideas work, not for reasons they won't. Do everything with enthusiasm, it's contagious.

— IAN PERCY

"Laughter is a celebration of the human spirit."

Fun is fundamental.

— DOUG HALL

Fun is the reward for working hard.
Celebrating together as a team
makes it all worthwhile.

— CHERYL WILLIAMS

A company that has fun, where
employees lunch with each other,
put cartoons on the wall, and celebrate,
is spirited, creative and usually profitable.

— DAVID BAUM

**If you're working in an organization
that is NOT enthusiastic, energetic, creative,
clever, curious, and just plain
fun, you've got serious troubles.**

— TOM PETERS

**What is central to business
is the joy of creating.**

— PETER ROBINSON

Creativity is inventing, experimenting,
growing, taking risks, breaking rules,
making mistakes, and having fun.

— MARY LOU COOK

The supreme achievement is to blur
the line between work and play.

— ARTHUR TOYNBEE

**Customers love people who have
fun doing their job. It's a contagious
effect which makes the service experience
unforgettably positive for us all.**

— BETH DRAKE

Each morning, see the movie
in your mind's eye of the kind of day
you envision for yourself, both job
is the job that relates to you
—JOHN MAXWELL MUSIC

"Honor and celebrate

Whether we are during the weld lights I
often project on celebrating an individual or
a company who's in that that only at earlier
tasks, I enjoy whatever you do the enjoy to honor.
Everyone enjoys to obtain work like most—
their purpose in their work.
—TOM PICKETT

the differences!"

— MARK DAVID

That which is to be most admired in America is oneness and not sameness. Sameness is the worst thing that could happen to the people of this country.

— RABBI STEPHEN S. WISE

What if we could learn to celebrate the wonderful, rich differences among people? Wouldn't a corporation that could tap the uniqueness of each of its employees be phenomenally powerful?

— TOM PETERS

Discover what is unique, what is great about people and honor it, be happy for it, use it.

— JOHN BUNN

Brilliance comes in all colors, strengths in many forms. When we learn to honor the differences and appreciate the mix, we're on our way.

— **KELLY ANN ROTHAUS**

**Wise leaders know that if
an individual doesn't count,
the company or organization
doesn't count for much either.**

— DIANE DREHER

Every individual matters.
Every individual has a role to play.
Every individual makes a difference.

— MOTTO OF THE JANE GOODALL INSTITUTE

Originality exists in every individual because each of us differs from the other. We are all prime numbers divisible only by ourselves.

— JEAN GUITTON

Each person wants a voice in human freedom—the freedom to express our individuality in work and life. That's a fire burning inside all of us.

— LECH WALESA

**I believe the highest form
of praise you can give any individual
is sincere and simple respect.**

— CAROL TRAMONTANA

The best companies assume that
each individual wants to make
a difference in the world and
be respected. Is that a surprise?

— PAUL AMES

Diversity is a competitive advantage. Different people approach similar problems in different ways.

— RICH MCGINN

Seeking diversity automatically leads us to excellence, just as focusing on excellence inevitably leads us to diversity.

— WILLIAM C. STEERE

"Celebrate your humanness. Celebrate your craziness. Celebrate your uniqueness. But celebrate you!"

**We are each gifted in a unique
and important way. It is our privilege
and our adventure to continually
discover our own special light.**

— MARY DUNBAR

Insist on being yourself. No one can
do that better than you, and no one can
ever tell you you're doing it wrong.

— JAMES COLLIER

There are many wonderful things
that will never be done if you
do not do them.

— CHARLES D. GILL

———————————

**You have a gift that only you can give
to the world—that's the whole reason
you're on the planet. The miracle of your
existence calls for celebration every day.**

— OPRAH WINFREY

**Dreams don't come true by themselves.
Goals aren't achieved by accident.
Planning is the 'how' of your life.**

— DAN ZADRA

Bringing out your own unique brand
of creativity into your life and the world can
be the most significant thing you'll ever do.

— LORNA CATFORD

When you do what you do best you
are helping not only yourself but the world.

— ROGER WILLIAMS

**You have a unique message to deliver,
a unique song to sing, a unique act of love
to bestow. This message, this song, and this
act of love have been entrusted exclusively
to the one and only you.**

— JOHN POWELL

The place you are in needs you today.

— KATHERINE LOGAN

I believe that one of the most important things to learn in life is that you can make a difference in your community no matter who you are or where you live.

— ROSALYNN CARTER

What you will do matters.
All you need is to do it.

— JUDY GRAHN

In a nation of millions, and a world of billions, the individual is still the first and basic agent of change.

— LYNDON JOHNSON

"Celebrate the one who thinks of others when all others are thinking of themselves."

No one was ever honored for what he received. Honor has been the reward for what he gave.

— CALVIN COOLIDGE

We are here to add what we can to, not to get what we can from, life.

— SIR WILLIAM OSLER

I must admit that I personally measure success in terms of the contributions an individual makes to his or her fellow human beings.

— MARGARET MEAD

Forget yourself for others, and others will never forget you.

— UNKNOWN

**Each of us has a choice about
how to love the world
in our own unique way.**

— BERNIE SIEGEL

There are souls in this world who have
the gift of finding joy everywhere—and leaving
it behind them when they go.

— FREDERICK WILLIAM FABER

There are two kinds of people—
those who come into a room and say,
'Well, here I am!' and those who come
in and say, 'Ah, there you are.'

— FREDERICK L. COLLINS

**The person we all love is the one
who's coming in the door when
everybody else is going out.**

— MASON COOLEY

Some people strengthen our society just by being the kind of people they are.

— JOHN GARDNER

The impersonal hand of government can never replace the helping hand of a neighbor.

— HUBERT HUMPHREY

Nothing liberates our greatness like
the desire to help, the desire to serve.

— MARIANNE WILLIAMSON

**America is great because she is good,
and if America ever ceased to be good,
America will cease to be great.**

— **ALEXIS DE TOCQUEVILLE**

"It's time for us all to stand and cheer for the doer—the one who recognizes the challenge and does something about it."

To begin is the most important part of any quest, and by far the most courageous.

— PLATO

Celebrate the one who went ahead and did the thing that everyone else merely talked about.

— MARK DAVID

**A great pleasure in life is doing
what people say you cannot do.**

— WALTER GAGEHOT

Do just once what everyone else
says cannot be done, and you will never
listen to the naysayers again.

— EDMUND BROWN

Take risks.
You can't fall off the bottom.

— BARBARA PROCTOR

**To get profit without risk,
experience without danger, and
reward without work, is as impossible
as it is to live without being born.**

— KEN HAKUTA

All the beautiful sentiments in the world weigh less than a single lovely action.

— JAMES RUSSELL LOWELL

You can either take action, or you
can hang back and hope for a miracle.
Miracles are great, but they
are too unpredictable.

— PETER DRUCKER

Our doubts are traitors, and make us lose the good we oft might win, by fearing the attempt.

— WILLIAM SHAKESPEARE

Nothing splendid has ever been achieved except by those who dared believe that something inside them was superior to circumstances.

— BRUCE BARTON

"Blue ribbon sales and service people are easily among your company's greatest assets and champions. Honor them. Celebrate them. Reward them."

— JIM WILLIAMSON

**The essential difference in service
is not machines or 'things.'
The essential difference is minds,
hearts, spirits, and souls.**

— HERB KELLEHER

Techniques don't produce quality
products and services; people do, people
who care, people who are treated as
creatively contributing individuals.

— TOM PETERS

A satisfied customer is the very best business strategy of all.

— MICHAEL LEBOEUF

If we make our customers important, they will inevitably return the favor.

— VINCE PFAFF

There is not a selling system in the world that can match the elegance, honesty and raw power of a great client relationship.

— **RICHARD ABRAHAM**

Just because the transaction is done,
that doesn't mean the relationship is over.

— MARTY RODRIGUEZ

The spirit of great sales and service
does not come from a manual,
it comes from the heart.

— DEBBI FIELDS

**We run this business with our hearts,
and we show it every chance we get.
It's not our culture to be complacent
in dealing with a customer.**

— NORMAN MAYNE

It is the service we are not obliged to give that people value the most.

— **JAMES C. PENNEY**

Everything extra that we voluntarily give to our customers comes back to us in terms of reputation, loyalty, referrals and praise. It not only feels good to surprise and pamper our customers, it's also smart business.

— MICHAEL NOLAN

The true value of a service or product is not what you put into it—it is what your customer gets out of it.
If your customer profits, you profit.

— PETER DRUCKER

Our customers will begin to realize that they really can count on faster, crisper, more caring and personal sales and service from us. That special relationship translates into real value for our customers. And when our customers win, we win.

— MARK DAVID

"The praise that comes from those

means the most
who know us best."

— DENNIS JOHNSON

There is nothing better than the encouragement of a good friend or teammate.

— **KATHERINE HATHAWAY**

There are many compliments that may come to an individual in the course of a lifetime, but there is no higher tribute than to be loved and appreciated by those who know us best.

— DALE E. TURNER

There is a peculiar gratification in receiving congratulations from one's squadron for a victory in the air.
It is worth more to a pilot than the applause of the whole outside world.

— EDDIE RICKENBACKER

The highest honor I have ever attained is that of having my name coupled with my troops in these great events.

— **GENERAL GEORGE S. PATTON**

**Those with whom we work
look to us for heat as well as light.**

— WOODROW WILSON

Each of us has a spark of life inside us,
and our highest endeavor ought to be
to set off that spark in one another.

— KENNY AUSUBEL

People work together because they need each other, and they also need to hear victories about each other.

— BILL MILLIKEN

Encourage each other to become the best you can be. Celebrate what you want to see more of.

— TOM PETERS

**You are not only good yourself,
but the cause of goodness in others.**

— SOCRATES

If your actions inspire others
to dream more, learn more, do more
and become more, you are a leader.

— JOHN QUINCY ADAMS

People will forget what you said,
people will forget what you did,
but people will never forget
how you made them feel.

— MAYA ANGELOU

**Enthusiasm reflects confidence,
spreads good spirit, raises morale,
arouses loyalty, and laughs at adversity.
It is beyond price.**

— ALLAN COX

"Celebrate those who attempt great things, even though they fail."

— SENECA

Honor and praise excellent failures!

— MARK DAVID

We are not going to succeed in everything we attempt in life. That's a guarantee. In fact, the more we do in life, the more chance there is not to succeed in some things.

— SUSAN JEFFERS

All have disappointments,
all have times when it isn't worthwhile.
— JOHN H. HANSON

Strength and courage aren't always measured in medals and victories. They are measured by the number of struggles and setbacks that must be weathered along the way.

— CAROL O'REILLY

"In the end the
recognition you
is your

most important
will ever receive
own."

— DOROTHY MAGUIRE

**There is an applause superior
to that of the multitude—one's own.**

— ELIZABETH ELTON SMITH

Of all the judgments you pass, none is so
important as the one you pass on yourself.

— NATHANIEL BRANDEN

A great life is the sum total
of all the worthwhile things
you've been doing one by one.

— RICHARD BACH

**When we're in our nineties and
we're looking back, it's not going to
be how much money we made or how
many awards we've won. It's really,
'What did we stand for? Did we make a
positive difference for people?'**

— ELIZABETH DOLE

Hats off to the past.
Coats off to the future.

— AMERICAN PROVERB

Develop an attitude of gratitude, and give thanks for everything that has happened to you, knowing that every step forward is a step towards achieving something bigger and better.

— BRIAN TRACY

My hope still is to leave the world
a bit better than when I got here.

— JIM HENSON

**Celebrate what you've
accomplished, but raise the bar a
little higher each time you succeed.**

— MIA HAMM

There is no finish line.

— NIKE MOTTO

I look at victory as a temporary milestone on a very long highway.

— JOAN BENOIT SAMUELSON

Celebrate today, knowing that new possibilities and adventures are just around the corner, and you will be ready for them.

— MARK DAVID

Let yourself re-graduate every four years. Celebrate what you have done. Admit what you are not doing. Think about what is important to you and make some changes. If you give yourself a chance to move on, you can do anything.

— CATHY GUISEWITE

"Treasure this day and treasure yourself. Truly, neither will ever happen again."

— RAY BRADBURY

**If you woke up today,
it's time to celebrate.**

— UNKNOWN

Normal day, let me be aware of the treasure you are. Let me learn from you, love you, bless you before you depart. Let me not pass you by in the quest of some rare and perfect tomorrow.

— MARY IRION

I wake each morning with the thrill
of expectation and the joy of being truly alive.
And I'm thankful for this day.

— ANGELA WOZNIAK

**This is the gift—to have the wonderful
capacity to appreciate again and again,
freshly and naively, the basic goods of life,
with awe, pleasure and wonder.**

— ABRAHAM MASLOW

**Every day may not look good,
but there is something good in every
day . . . if you will only stop to look.**

— GARY MEDICA

My goal has always been not
to look forward to the next thing,
but to fully relish and celebrate the
things of this moment, this day.

— DIANNA AGRON

Whatever I'm doing at
the moment is the biggest thing in life—
whether it is conducting a symphony
or peeling an orange.

— ARTURO TOSCANINI

**Make something every day.
Make a song, make a move,
make a friend, make a buck,
make a difference.**

— PAT COLLELO

We tend to forget that happiness doesn't come as a result of getting something we don't have, but rather in recognizing and celebrating what we do have.

— FREDERICK KOENIG

Take time each day to appreciate all the wonderful things that money can't buy— the wind in your hair, the sun on your face, meaningful work, a child's laughter, a loving family, a great friend.

— DAN ZADRA

It would be foolish to postpone enjoyment of everyday life until you are more successful, more secure, or more loved than you are today.

— TIMOTHY RAY MILLER

Celebrate the happiness that friends are always giving. Make every day a holiday, and celebrate just living.

— **AMANDA BRADLEY**